Loved it! Without pretense, the author draws from her life experiences and distills them into a primer for living. A keen observer, she finds learning opportunities in everyday life, which she harnesses for her own growth. "Living the questions" seems to come naturally and she employs the answers in her life. Looking for the good in others. Willing to hear answers that sometimes surprise, but always contribute to her appreciation of others. The use of woodcut-style images underscores her focus on fundamental truths. I wholeheartedly encourage you to have a look!

 Gary Spangler

You hold in your hand a bunch of little wisdoms. Take this opportunity to delve into delight. You may learn something useful to you, or not, but either way you will enjoy the experience.

 Stuart James

Reading Gail Boenning is like sitting and listening to an old friend... whom you have not actually met yet. But still you

*laugh, you ponder, and occasionally your allergies kick in a
little so you have to wipe your eyes and blow your nose.*

Jack Herlocker

"I met a Puppy as I went walking;
   We got talking,
   Puppy and I.
   'Where are you going this nice fine day?'
    (I said to the Puppy as he went by).
   'Up to the hills to roll and play.'
   'I'll come with you, Puppy', said I."
~A. A. Milne "Puppy and I"

*I have been following Gail for several years and I can easily
say I have watched her grow as a writer. Many of her
stories are told through her muses and many are about her
love for her four-legged friend Henrietta. She passes her
knowledge on to us with great wisdom. I know you will
enjoy reading this as Gail has such deep insights into this
thing called life. You will find yourself feeling as if you are
part of her family as you read of her adventures with
husband, son, and Henny.*

Monty Bates

Gail's writings convey the experience of sitting in a most comfortable setting and enjoying conversation with a good friend. The resonance of her voice, her authenticity, and her curious and good-hearted nature are woven into nourishing meals, each chapter an invitation into savoring learning through the arc of life's individual stories as they interweave to create the tapestry of a lifetime. In this way, both readers who are in their youthful or later adventures can feel enriched in discoveries and reflections of the wisdom embodied within these and within their own stories. A deeper satisfaction with your own journey is warmly at hand.

Gary Breads — Wisdom Sailing School

Gail Boenning's Wandering Words invites the reader with calm yet friendly energy to see every tiny moment in a fresh new light. It could be at the grocery check-out lane, looking at an old photograph, chance connections with strangers, or even from the muses in your head. You can call her philosophy everyday mindfulness, or you can just appreciate the pauses and in-between moments Gail highlights in this collection for opportunities to learn, appreciate and grow. The gift of Wandering Words is after you read it, you will start to see the world in colorful ABCs all around you — and you can start today.

Tim Cigelske — Author of The Creative Journey

WANDERING WORDS

WANDERING WORDS

A WALK FROM A TO Z

GAIL BOENNING

Editor: Noosha Ravaghi

Cover Sketch: Anya Toomre

Cover Design: Nathaniel Dasco

Photography: Gail Boenning

Photo to Sketch Conversion: Clip2Comic

For ...

Elsa—who accepted my learning with grace
Mara—who excelled at giving and receiving unconditional love
Henrietta—who models presence, curiosity, and adventure
be here now

"Dogs have a way of finding the people who need them, and filling an emptiness we didn't ever know we had. "
~Thom Jones

INTRODUCTION

*F*rom the library shelf it whispered, "Pick me."

Who was I to refuse such a request? For books had chosen me a time or two before and changed me for the better. And so it was that *The Wander Society* by Keri Smith and I traveled home together.

I saw myself within the pages of a book filled with wisdom on walking and self-awareness. I have been wandering almost daily from an early age, often with a *four-leg* by my side. Falling into reverie while surrounded by nature affords me space to explore the content of my mind.

> *Who are you? Why do you think that? Where did that idea come from? Why are you afraid? What do you love? Who might you become?*

In the spring of 2016, I came across a writing challenge...100 Naked Words.

I was intrigued...*could I write 100 words per day? What would I say? What might come of it?*

I began with a sorry little story that wore all my labels —name, age, marital status, nationality and occupation (or lack thereof). The first two paragraphs of the post showed a tiny flame of potential though:

> *Here goes nothing, or possibly everything, as I offer up my first post to 100 Naked Words. I would like to thank Johnson for allowing me to contribute to what promises to be an interesting collection of work.*
>
> *I am starting today with some simple demographic facts to give the reader some insight into my writing perspective. It is NOT my goal to "help" anyone. It IS my goal to offer a viewpoint that is uniquely mine. Some*

will agree and others will not, but I hope all readers will try to see the world as I see it. Empathy is underrated.

I'd set out on an unexpected road of transformation, changing my life, and therefore the lives of others. A woman who didn't think she had a creative bone in her body found a few.

These twenty-six essays are a random sampling of my writing over the last five years. The style, sentiments, and writing skill level vary from piece to piece. My hope is that you'll find a thought, or 26, that inspire you to ask yourself some questions about who you are and how you dance with the river of thoughts flowing through you.

I am grateful you are here.

"But it isn't Easy," said Pooh . . . "Because Poetry and Hums aren't things which you get, they're things which get you. And all you can do is go to where they can find you." ~A. A. Milne

 *an invitation to pause and share*

ACCEPT DIFFERENCES

Accepting differences
Seems an obvious thing to do,
For not one single person, not even a twin,
Is exactly like you.

Exterior variances are obvious to the eye;
It takes an open heart and mind
To see what's going on inside

Does not always match

The reality you think you see.

Each person's story is different
I am not you;
You are not me.

I might bristle at your (hi)story
Grating against my sensitivities
Bumpity-bumping with my memories.

Best course...Do not resist.
Seek understanding.
With questions do persist.

It takes two to arrive
On common ground.

Never impossible
Is what I have found...

You can choose acceptance
Over anger and despair,
Shift to a different shore.

Life's gifts have never been fair.

Your internal landscape is what you control.
If we could all grasp this,
A light would shine from every soul.

Perhaps the maker's plan was thus...
Explore how me *is part of* us.

Variety abounds...
Accepting differences
Is where love is found.

Accept Differences

BE KIND

*W*aiting for my cart full of broccoli, chicken thighs, potato chips, frozen cherries, and bottled tea to be scanned, I eavesdropped on a conversation between a mother and a teen...

"Mrs. Olsen was looking at the long list of kids dropping her class for second semester today. She came over and told me she was disappointed to see my name on the list."

"Oh?"

"From September until January, she lost three of my assignments — each submitted on time. On every assignment that was not multiple choice, I received an 89%. She never mixed it up — 87, 91, 85, 93. Always 89. Does she even read my work?"

"Welcome to life," said the mom. "You can discuss your grievances with Mrs. Olsen or you can keep your head down and take your B. It's also up to you whether or not you drop her class second semester."

"There's an online form to submit course feedback."

"Are you going to fill it out?" the mom asked.

"Maybe."

"Well, you have choices. You can be mean, nice, or kind," the mother said.

To raised eyebrows she continued, "*Mean* is obvious. *Nice* is glossing over — or ignoring the form altogether. *Kind* is giving honest feedback because you care about the students she has after you. What if you tell her what she could have done differently to engage your interest and keep you in your seat?"

Who knew the grocery checkout line could also be a classroom?

Be Kind

COUNT YOUR BLESSINGS

$\mathcal{W}$hen my beloved Labrador Mara was a pup, somebody gifted her a bag of locally made doggy treats. In bold letters, inside a big, red star, the label announced: *Only 3 calories per treat!*

Charlee Bear: For Training or Just For Fun — The Treat You Can Give Often

Eleven years later, Mara continues to gobble the round rewards like a three-year-old with a rocket pop. Flavored with real cheese and turkey, cranberries and sweet potatoes, the goodies look like oyster crackers.

Charlee Bear helped us train Mara to sit, stay and come.

Counting your blessings is like treating your mind with Charlee Bear treats — *calorie free!*

Gratitude: For Training or Just For Fun — The Treat You Can Give Often

Count Your Blessings

4

DREAM

*W*hat happens when we receive the dream we didn't know we dreamt?

Back when I wore ankle length skirts and flat shoes with toes resembling arrowheads, I dreamed of leaving small town life and taking big cities by storm. I dreamed of commutes among tall buildings, bustling streets, and sophisticated nightlife. I thought I wanted a high powered job in a fancy business suit.

Where'd that dream come from?

Did movies when I was a young adult portray high powered women in business suits taking big cities by storm?

Hmmm...I remember a film with Diane Keaton. She traded in her heels to go make baby food in the country. Jane, Lily, and Dolly worked 9 to 5 and Melanie Griffith was a Working Girl.

At a small university I listened to professors lecture on history, law, communication, and the Spanish language. The town was very much like the one I grew up in, surrounded by forests and corn fields. There I met my future husband. He grounded me and held the promise of something I didn't even know I was looking for...

After graduation, I landed a job in Wisconsin's largest city and even though I didn't have a windowed corner office requiring an elevator lift, I was building a beautiful life. Synchronicity linked me with a lifelong friend who remarkably lived in the same apartment complex I moved into. For years we shared a commute across the busy interstate between our homes and jobs in the same office.

I got married and we remodeled a duplex before building the home we live in today. I became a mother and enjoy long walks with my Labrador, living a life free from the daily grind. I learned how to grow a garden and bake pies from scratch. None of this was in my adolescent dream...*or was it? Hiding somewhere behind what I thought I was supposed to want?*

By all means *dream* — but remain open to what happens moment to moment.

As someone once said, *Life is what happens when you're busy making other plans.*

Dream

5

EXPRESS THANKS

*a*s I drove toward the library from our financial planner's office, my cell rang through the Bluetooth speaker.

"Hi Dad!"

"You staying warm? This is good ice making

weather!"

"Yes, Dad, I'm in the truck and I have the heated seat on."

"Oh, isn't that nice? Great invention."

Dad was calling to report on Sturgeon Bay's thickening ice. Grandfather, grandson, and perhaps the mother in the middle most of all, had their fingers crossed for a generational ice fishing adventure.

Every time I talk to my dad these days, he reminds me he could '*go at any time*'... He's 82.

Our conversation traveled to Dad's dental concerns. He referenced root canals, pulled teeth, dental implants, and medical invoices over the past several weeks. My frugal and practical dad has decided to accept a root canal and partial bridge to fill in for missing teeth. He chose the least expensive solution.

"I might only get six months out of it. Why would I spend $15,000 when I can get by spending $3000? Rather you kids get the money."

He went on, "You know George Washington had false teeth?"

"Yeah, they were made out of wood, right?" I asked.

"Can you imagine how their breath smelled?"

I didn't want to get into it with my dad on the phone, but I can imagine what George Washington's mouth smelled like. Our old Lab Retriever Mara has had dental issues for most of her life. She had her first tooth pulled at age three and she is down to less than half the choppers she started life with — the other half pulled.

The old girl is all bark and no bite.

Despite numerous attempts to brush her teeth with meat flavored toothpaste, spiking her water with blue dental aid, regular six month cleanings, and insane amounts of antibiotics, Mara's mouth often smells like...*use your imagination.* Her condition, called Stomatitis, has worsened significantly over the last year. I feel guilty for keeping my distance and cringing when she brings her face close to mine.

Over the years, three different veterinarians cleaned, pulled, and prescribed the common dog antibiotic for oral infections. I'm thankful for all the care Mara received, but it's to veterinarian #4 that I'm sending a card and chocolates.

Dr. Thompson drew the lucky straw to clean Mara's teeth in November. I am sooooo thankful!

In addition to scraping and polishing, she treated Mara's gums with a laser, cleaned her ears, and looked for any identifiable causes of the persistent decay problem. When I picked Mara up, Dr. Thompson said, "I'll reach out to some specialists and check some of the online veterinary boards to see what I can find out."

The holidays came and went. In January, everyone in our house was keeping their distance from Mara again. Mara was drooling, yawning, and rubbing her face on the furniture and floor. *Was the poor girl experiencing more mouth pain?*

Oh, how I love this dog who has been a loyal friend and companion for eleven years!

I scheduled a follow-up appointment with Dr. Thompson. She looked in Mara's mouth and confirmed her gums were again ulcerated.

"Let me take a culture and investigate some more," she said.

Within a week, Dr. Thompson called with a new plan of action.

She prescribed a new antibiotic that seems to be working. Within twelve hours, I was going nose to nose with my girl. Mara continues to yawn and rub her snout, but thanks to Dr. Thompson's tenacity, I feel we're moving forward.

As Maya Angelou said, *"People remember how you make them feel."*

Dr. Thompson's curiosity and willingness to step beyond the obvious made me feel seen and heard.

Filled with gratitude, I'll express my thanks.

Express Thanks

6

FORGIVE

$\mathscr{E}$ight-year-old Ellie flopped into the chair. She pulled her knees up to her chest and crossed her arms on top. The corners of her mouth melted toward her chin.

Ellie's ten-year-old brother, Ethan, threw himself

onto his bed. He picked up their Border Collie's tennis ball and thumped it against his closed door — once, twice, three times...

"Enough!" Mrs. Comenity yelled from the kitchen.

Poor Elliot paced around the open concept first floor. Raised voices with an edge unnerved the sensitive dog. He scratched at the front door, hoping to be let out.

Mrs. Comenity called her children to the dining table.

"What is going on?" she asked. "Do you see how your mood is upsetting Elliot? And...me?"

"Ellie broke my Lego ship!"

"I twisted my ankle on it because you left it right outside my bedroom door!"

"You should watch where you're walking!"

"Hold the phone!" interrupted Mrs. Comenity. "Let's all take a breath...."

Ethan rolled his eyes and whispered to Ellie, "Here we go again — Mindful Mom to the rescue."

"I can hear you," Mrs. Comenity said — eyes twinkling despite her pursed lips. "Ellie, can you still walk?"

"Ummmm...yeah."

"Ethan can you rebuild your ship?"

"Maybe, but I'd rather use some of the pieces for the football field I'm building."

"OK then. You can choose to be angry, or you can

forgive each other and we can enjoy game night when Dad gets home...I know what Elliot wants you to choose."

Forgiveness...an exercise in moving forward.

Forgive

7

GIVE FREELY

he longer I live, the more I recognize the real zest of life lives in the little, everyday gestures of presence — a smile shared while in line at the post office, a generous massage of an old dog's limbs, a listening ear tuned and receptive. Such giving lifts us up out of our own mind's shenanigans.

Our flavors meld and spread throughout the pot —
sweet, spicy, salty, savory or bitter.

Give freely, mindful of your addition.

———

The tiny photo was taken over twenty years ago and
represents timeless beauty — a cat basking on an open
window sill. I've never been a student of photography,
but my layman's eyes are drawn in by sunlight
streaming over a hanging plant, radiating on to create a
halo around Samantha, the Tabby.

I remember...

Samantha was the first pet I called mine. We
owned each other. As a kitten, she was devilish. She
climbed curtains and bare legs. At the age of twenty-
three, she was a restless bag of bones. The years in
between carried moments of *isn't she adorable* and *why
is she so naughty.*

The window faced east, from the spare bedroom of
the first home I owned. The view looked out into the
tiniest of backyards, with a garden that supplied more
produce than we could eat. Our first dog, Elsa, was a
pro at picking her own tomatoes and green peppers.
She always ate what she picked and we found joy in
her odd behavior — a story to tell.

There's the tiniest hint of red visible on the
hanging planter, reminding me of my friend Barbara.
One day, while she questioned me about something at

my desk, she said, "What a lovely photo! Every photo should contain a little bit of red." She must have felt this was important because Barbara was reluctant to discuss anything but work, at work. Why'd she believe that?

To this day, when I take a picture, I always look to include something red.

One small photo gifts many memories.

Sometimes less is more.

Give Freely

HARM NO ONE

*O*hhhhh, this one is tough...there is a fine line between help and harm.

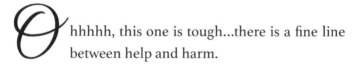

I had a conversation with Mr. Grosbeak...

"Hello...a refill please?" he chirped.

"Hmmmm...we need to talk about your love affair with grape jelly my friend. You're here when I get up in the morning. You're here at dusk when I'm cleaning up the

kitchen. You gobble, gobble, gobble. I crank the casement and squeeze the sticky purple dispenser several times per day. Orioles have stopped snacking...can't recall the last time I saw your mate. You alone are emptying the jelly cups." I replied.

My family's started calling him The Addict. Something seems wrong — all that grape flavored corn syrup cannot be good for the rose-breasted beauty. Where is his feathered flock? Will he remember how to forage? What'll happen when we go on vacation and his jelly supply is cut off?

"So, uhhh...I looked it up...and while the aviary experts say a little bit of grape jelly won't hurt you, you need to scavenge beyond my window. As much as I'll miss your beauty and companionship, I'm cutting you down to two jelly glops per day. When it's gone, it's gone. Now go eat some cherries and mosquitoes, will you? Haven't you heard variety is the spice of life?"

Two days later, Mr. Grosbeak continues to land on the feeder and blink at me through the window, but I think he's catching on. He's not here as often, and, once he finds the feeder empty, he flies off. I've also stopped filling the seed feed as there's an abundance of fresh kernels, fruits and insects to fuel the fliers this time of year.

Sometimes, even when acting with the best of intentions, I create problems instead of solutions.

A wise teen once told me, "It's called life. We mess up and we learn."

Harm No One

9

IMAGINE MORE

*C*lose your eyes... Wait, that will make it impossible to read.

Instead... take a deep breath... so deep you can feel your lower back expand... and let it out like honey pouring from a jar, slow and sweet.

Imagine you're eight years old on the playground.

Joyfully you run, hop, and skip. You plop your tiny bottom onto a swing. Scrawny legs pump forward and back.

You feel like you're flying!

Satisfied, you drag your sneakered feet like landing gear, with zero regard for your shoe's wellbeing.

The metal play structure calls your name. You clamber like a ladybug on the kitchen wall headed for the ceiling. Whooshing down the fireman's pole, you slide so fast you land on your butt instead of your feet.

Undeterred — body and spirit hop up and start running again.

A bell blares. Somebody somewhere has decided recess is over. You must get in line, stay quiet, and march back indoors.

Where does your greatest potential lie — playground or classroom?

The answer is not one size fits all.

Imagine More

10

JETTISON WORRY

*D*o you talk to yourself as much as I do?

When I was growing up, my father talked to himself — *out loud*. My mom, siblings and I used to tease him. He'd be in the basement working on a project and we'd hear, "Now where is that hammer?"

"Who is your father talking to?" Mom would ask.

"Himself!" one of us would reply and we'd all start giggling. He teased us right back — told us he was the most reasonable person he knew.

"I've got a lot I can learn from myself!" he'd say.

I no longer think talking to oneself is funny or crazy. Most often, I keep my inner chatter under my hat with the volume muted. My self-to-self conversations contribute more to my life story than any outside circumstance ever could.

Thoughtful conversations with myself help me to respond like a summer breeze rather than react like a thunderstorm.

For example, last night I went to dinner and The Addams Family musical with a friend. As we were leaving the restaurant I opened my purse, wanting to take a quick peek at my phone. "Wait. My phone. I have to go back inside," I told my friend. "I must have taken my cell out with my wallet and left it on the table."

I checked with the hostess and the young waitstaff who'd bussed our table. "Sorry, no phone," they told me.

I consulted with myself and made a choice not to fret.

Whew!

I'd printed paper copies of the tickets I'd purchased online. Every time my mind wanted to jump into a negative loop of *where could it be, are you losing your mind? or you've only paid a couple of months toward that mini, life-line, purse computer — how could you lose it?*

another internal voice would counter, *it's just a thing, you probably left it on the kitchen counter; now just **stop it**, be quiet and enjoy the show.*

The second voice prevailed and I stood strong in the present moment — entertained by dedicated kids who sang and acted their hearts out on opening night.

When I got home and entered the laundry room from the garage, a rested and relaxed, black, rectangular genie sat quietly on the washing machine. I think my phone enjoyed the night off.

And my night ended as happily as the Addams family's.

Jettison Worry

11

KINDLE CONNECTIONS

*W*hat happens when *1+1* equals a sum greater than two?

Magical Math

Despite my well-worn, grey, pleats-near-the-shoulders, hooded sweatshirt, I was cold in the hospital waiting room. I saw blue sky and sunlight through the windows looking out into the parking lot. Outside the temperature was in the mid eighties, but my bare legs were covered in goosebumps. I'd rushed out of the house in my running shorts. We'd already been at the hospital for several hours — long enough for the air conditioned chill to reach my bones. I flipped the pages of a food magazine and found myself drawn in by a farmers' market quiz.

Of course I know what a ramp is! No, a chive is not an onion. Iceberg is the mildest lettuce. Purslane — the weed that's a delicacy — I wrote about purslane once!

Here's one I was stuck on: What is the proper name for a fruit that's a cross between an apricot and a plum?

a.) pluot

b.) aprium

c.) plumcot

d.) apriplum

The answer key on page 65 solved the mystery — e.) all of the above.

1 plum + 1 apricot = 6 different fruits! (plum, apricot, pluot, aprium, plumcot, apriplum)

Zipping my sweatshirt to my chin and rubbing my arms for heat, I thought of an article I'd recently read in Aeon magazine about philosopher David Hume — one particular sentence stuck with me and my mind connected the dots:

So you can prove 2 + 2 = 4 but that tells you nothing about what happens when you put four things together in nature, where they could obliterate each other, multiply or merge into one.

Bending down to double tie my strong-willed shoe laces — they frequently untie themselves — I thought more about the conversation I'd just been a part of in the patient's room. I sat on the stool with wheels because the doctor didn't need it. A monitor above the patient's bed constantly flashed blood pressure, heart rate and oxygen saturation readings. Sometimes it beeped.

Curly black hair, kind face and approachable manner, the respiratory therapist offered a warm contrast to the antiseptic room. She entered and explained that the medication recently administered during the patient's breathing treatment was a mix of two separate drugs.

"You'd think one plus one equals two," she said. "But with these medicines combined, you really get three. Combining them creates a third property that makes them even more effective. Make sense? Do you have the power combo for your home inhaler?" she asked.

Despite a pager call and another hospital employee seeking her assistance, the respiratory therapist answered all of our questions with the patience of Mother Theresa. She didn't leave until she felt we fully understood the equipment, medication, at-home strategies, and follow-up protocol. Then, after a gentle well wish, she was on her way down the corridor to perform magical math with another patient.

When she left the room, the patient said, "I learned more from her in ten minutes than I did after years of doctors' visits."

The respiratory therapist, through her patient efforts, transformed what could have been a simple provider/patient conversation into something bigger. She'd pulled off the magic of 1+1=3. The conversation she made time for effectively eased the patient's mind — a gift of love and compassion.

I'm now wiggling in my chair, anxious to get up and move a bit. Even though it's still an unseasonably warm 85 degrees four days later, I have a blanket over my shoulders in our air-conditioned house. I get chilly whenever I sit still.

I've reached the point in my story where I could use a little help. Like all Olympic gymnasts, I like my stories best when I stick the landings. A recent read of *The War of Art* by Steven Pressfield has me consulting my muses. Real or imagined, muses are excellent coaches.

Urania, Calliope, Thalia? Can you put down your popcorn and send me a closing thought to end this piece? Please?

"Isn't it obvious?" Calliope asks with her mouth full.

"Buber — I and Thou," Urania whispers.

Ahh, Martin Buber, the philosopher who wrote I

and Thou — a philosophy of relationship — the magical three formed when 1+1 makes room for one more — two together forming a relationship. One plus one equals three.

"Yes, that's it!" Thalia winks at me.

Magical Math — it's what I strive for with my words — you, me and our relationship makes three.

Kindle Connections

12

LIVE IN THE PRESENT

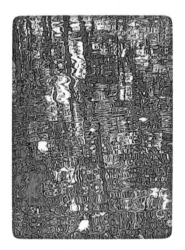

I wrote an entire essay — fidgeted and fussed over a quote from naturalist John Muir and connected his thoughts with mine across time and space.

I felt like a fifth grader on the final day of the

school year, finishing one last assignment before being released to play.

After a final read through, self-satisfaction might have been my undoing because one slip of the finger and computer gremlins erased every single word I'd written.

Anticipating a cruise on the Fox River in my single-man, sky-blue kayak, where I hoped to see herons, egrets, and turtles and to hear whinnies, snorts, and nickers, I was anxious to paddle past the paddocks of Thunder Bit Stables... *Was I doomed to stay indoors and begin again?*

After every consonant and vowel vanished, I couldn't bear to start over. I loaded up the truck with vessel, paddle, and life jacket.

Here I am, several hours later, refreshed and ready to write again.

On my trip upstream and then down I did not see the long, thin-legged egret or the massive, majestic heron. Not one single box turtle basked in my view. The horses were as quiet as church mice.

Instead, I saw carp surface and roll among water weeds. Cottonwood fluff floated through the air and on the water's surface. Dragonflies hovered and zoomed wearing iridescent shades of black, teal, and blue. Red-winged blackbirds chirped and called *conk-la-leeee*. I soaked in sight, sound, and feel.

What left the strongest impression, as an easterly wind rippled the reflection of a tree-lined shore, was the soft image pictured above, reminding me of Monet's Water Lilies.

Nature is a breeding ground for inspiration and peace.

> *"Climb the mountains and get their good tidings. Nature's peace will flow into you as sunshine flows into trees. The winds will blow their own freshness into you and the storms their energy, while cares will drop away from you like the leaves of autumn."* ~John Muir

Live in the Present

13

MASTER SOMETHING

I've been dancing with the concept of mastery.

I don't know about you, but I used to think that mastery was for others — *you know*, Olympic athletes, artists, Guinness Book record holders — the people who already achieved fame for their actions. *They make it look easy, don't they?*

What we often fail to see is the courage it took to start, along with the ups and downs along the way. We see finished products and think, *I could never do that.*

At the beginning, neither could they.

The recipe for the first pie crust I made came from *Betty Crocker's Picture Cookbook*. I refuse to blame Betty for years of scraping dough off my counters with a spatula and mending dough with floured fingers. I did the best I could with the famous home cook's instructions — try and try again.

After many years of practice, an article in a magazine offered me this trick: roll the dough between sheets of Saran wrap.

Wouldn't you know... it works like a charm.

Over the years I picked up additional pie craft tools and ideas. I purchased a pastry cutter instead of using two butter knives to cut shortening and flour together. I learned that using frigid ice water to bind ingredients makes a flakier end product.

My point?

I've been making pie crusts for over twenty years and I can say the original attempt looked nothing like the crusts of today. Mastery is a process of repetition and adjustment.

Mastery does not always end in fame or fortune. The courage to show up time and time again, attempting to produce results that match your vision with perseverance is the shell that holds sweetness.

> *"I still remember the shudder when I sensed a knowing as sure as fact—that I might only truly become my fullest self if I explored and stayed open to moving through daunting terrain."* ~Sarah Lewis

Master Something

14

NEST

*H*e was behind me at the Sherwin-
Williams checkout counter. I'd just
purchased four gallons of *Ranchero Red* deck stain and
the young woman behind the counter offered to carry
them to my car.

"Nah, I can get it, but thanks," I said.

Glenn picked up the box and said, "I'm gonna get that for you!"

I smiled and replied, "Okay. I'm going to let you," and as I held the door open for him, "My name is Gail."

"I'm Glenn. You can't beat this deck stain. I've been finishing and restoring decks for thirty years. There's nothing better."

"So, let me ask then, do you have any pointers? I've pressure washed and picked away at all of the peeling edges. Do I have to sand?"

I think I whined a little on that last question.

Guess what he replied...

You betcha!

Ugh!

Glenn suggested I sand... and purchase quality paint brushes... prime the bare spots... apply two light coats, one day apart from each other.

"Here's my card if you have any more questions."

I didn't tell Glenn I'd been to Home Depot for cheap paint brushes before stopping at the paint store.

Glenn's generosity made my day, even though I ignored his advice.

When you're expecting a baby, you nest. Sometimes you just don't have time for all of the steps.

Our newest family member was born on June 5th.

She has brown eyes, black fur and four paws. She'll be coming "home" in July.

To prepare for the new arrival, we've been weeding, mulching, and... now staining. Not because the pup will care, but because...

a.) how can one possibly get these big jobs done with a puppy underfoot, and

b.) once I start, I'm like a Lab with a tennis ball — go, go, go!

Nest

15

OPEN

$\mathcal{T}$his week I made some interesting person to person connections.

How are you?

For many of us, the question is a nicety. The phrase pops out on autopilot. *Fine* or *Busy* are typical responses, often spoken without intent to engage. Nothing wrong with using our manners, but I'd like to share three quick stories of conversations I had with strangers this week — toes dipping below the surface.

Each interaction left an impression on me. Maybe they'll touch you, too...

The connections remind me that in the course of a minute or two, we have so much power to leave a positive imprint on somebody.

On Monday, Mara barked ferociously when she heard the knock. I followed her into the laundry room, wrapped my arm around her chest so she couldn't run out into the garage, and opened the door. Talking over her gravelly, old dog woof I asked, "Are you okay with dogs?"

The man wearing work boots and a tool belt nodded his head up and down.

"Great, please come in out of the cold! Step into the kitchen where the sun is shining — warm up for a few minutes."

Rick had just fixed our garage door. Outside temperatures were in the single digits. "I appreciate it," he said.

"Do you have a dog?" I asked.

"Well, sort of...," he replied. "My ex-girlfriend and I — we unfortunately split up. She's got the dog. It's a mix between a chihuahua and a wiener dog — a chiweenie." I raised my eyebrows.

"She doesn't like the dog, but my kids wanted to keep it. I only see them every other weekend now. I feel bad."

"How old are your kids?" I asked.

"Ten and twelve. One started middle school this

year and the other is in... fourth grade, I think."

"What are their names?"

Rick told me, then volunteered, "I text them both every morning and every night — do my best to stay in touch."

"That's great," I said. "Keeping in contact is really important. I bet your kids look forward to those texts and calls. What do I owe you?"

Rick blinked and took a breath, "Oh yeah, ummm... we're doing electronic receipts now. Here's your total. I'll email you a copy."

———

On Tuesday after sharing a *hello*, the grocery checker asked me, "How are you? You know, we don't ask each other that enough." She stood still and waited for my answer.

"I'm great," I replied. "Fortunate to have a full cart of groceries and a checker asking how I am. *I think* we often ask each other how we are; we just don't really listen for an answer. We just keep moving — going about our business."

"Yeah, strangers just don't talk to each other much anymore. I can only do my part by trying. Look..."

She pulled up her sleeve to show me the Serenity Prayer tattooed on her arm.

God, grant me the serenity to accept the things I cannot

change, the courage to change the things I can, and wisdom to know the difference.

"Nice," I said. "I like the purple and blue accents."

"I read it every morning and every night," she said. Only then did she start pulling groceries from my cart.

On Wednesday, I stopped at the receptionist before heading to the parking lot with a new toothbrush, sample size toothpaste and mini dental floss dispenser.

"All set for today? Need anything from me?" I asked.

"All good," Cheryl said. "Have you been in any productions recently?"

I had to stop and think about that for a second. *What did she mean?* Outside of appointments and billing, we knew nothing about each other. *Had she seen me in a play years ago?*

It turned out, she had. We talked for over ten minutes about theater, creativity, her five children and two grandchildren, and her upcoming trip to Florida. The persistent ring of the phone put an end to our chatter. "I suppose I have to answer that," she said.

"See you in September."

Open

16

PACK LIGHTLY

The zipper of my backpack bulged. I opened the car door, went around the back of the vehicle and gave my niece a bear hug.

"Thank you — for everything! I had a great time — love you!"

She got back into her car and drove off while I took several deep breaths of Houston's warm, humid air.

After passing through the automatic, sliding glass doors, I slipped on my long sleeve athletic shirt, buttoned a favorite plaid flannel over the top and zipped up my black winter vest. Resting on my abdomen, underneath the layers, my purse was invisible to the United representative who verified I had only one perfectly sized carry-on bag.

The security line was short. While the TSA agent examined my driver's license, I slipped off my vest and tennis shoes. Hastily stuffing the license back into my purse, I pulled its strap over my head and piled it into the grey plastic bin with my shoes and vest.

"Step in," the agent instructed.

I raised my hands over my head per the blue stick person's outline and watched the vertical scanning bar circle in front of me.

"Step out," the agent instructed.

I could see my belongings just outside the x-ray machine. My grey bin rested on metal rollers waiting for a push from the bin behind.

I collected myself and my belongings in the recombobulation area. Shoes tied, purse hidden and vest zipped, I headed toward Gate 37.

Ohhhh — What's that over there? A glass case filled with tubs of ice cream?

"I'll have a single scoop of mint chip in a cake cone, please."

Five dollars lighter, my wallet and I took a seat near an electrical outlet. The flight was still on schedule and

I had a half hour before boarding. I checked my boarding pass for my seat number and found I'd not been assigned.

See Gate Agent my pass said.

Nate at the gate looked how you might expect an agent to look late on a Sunday afternoon.

"Sorry to disturb you," I said, "but my boarding pass indicates I need to see you?"

He looked up from his phone without a smile and started ruffling through a stack of passes.

"My son's name is Nate — really Nathaniel — that's what I call him." I said.

"Mine, too — and I never liked it," he said.

"Why not? It means 'Gift from God'."

"Yeah, I know that," Nate said, finally cracking a smile. "Don't anybody pronounce it right, though. I prefer Nate."

"Everybody my son has met since kindergarten calls him Nate, too. His kindergarten teacher sent home a note the second week of school — *Nathaniel would like to be called Nate at school* it read. Apparently she didn't have the time or patience to put up with nine letters of penmanship practice from my kid. I get it — he hated writing, still does."

"Here's your pass," Nate said.

Row 9 — Aisle seat

Pack Lightly

QUELL RUMORS

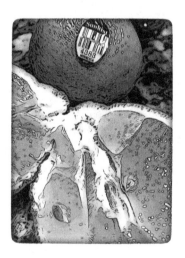

*a*n iridescent bubble sits at the tip of my tongue. Inside the globe, a half-formed story swirls.

I want to share what's traveled from somebody's

mouth to my ear, through my conscious and unconscious interpretations, with another link in the chain.

This gossip is crying for release.

A story is ready to burst forth like juice droplets spray from separated citrus segments.

Before releasing the orb, I consider adding embellishments and subtracting dull parts. Depending on the audience, I might say something like, *You didn't hear this from me* or *This doesn't leave this room* or *I might not have all of the facts exactly right* or *This is how I heard it...*

Stop! If I'm not willing or able to discuss with the real life characters of the story — **pop that bubble!**

"Strong minds discuss ideas, average minds discuss events, weak minds discuss people." ~Socrates

Quell Rumors

RECIPROCATE

*H*ave you ever performed a flanking maneuver at the grocery store? You smell the toothpick speared mini-sausages before you see the gentleman standing behind a display barrel. A banner announces *Locally Made — World's Best BBQ*.

Tiny white paper cups brimming with sauce ring the electric fry pan.

Avoiding eye contact, you skirt around the bunker that holds frozen chicken wings and shrimp.

You know if you try the Sauce King's sauce, your reciprocity reflex will muscle a jar right into your cart. And you don't like BBQ.

Or perhaps, you're a BBQ connoisseur and made a beeline to the barrel at first smell? You dip and munch, then stack bottles of sauce between your broccoli and bread.

The rule of reciprocation is drilled into us as children.

"There's not a single human culture that fails to train its members in this rule," author Robert Cialdini says.

Have you ever considered that whatever comes your way most likely has a relationship with what you're putting out?

Reciprocate

19

SCAFFOLD LEARNING

*I*t was early days...

I had no idea what I was doing.

I see that I did not attribute the photo I'd found over on Pexels to pair with my words all those years ago.

I remember feeling shame because I was aware other writers were giving credit where credit was due.

In time... I learned.

That's how my best life is lived... learning.

Everything I understand builds a scaffold for me to stand on and learn more.

The story read:

Tell me your story and I'll tell you mine.

Ok, that's not me, but I will probably look something like that in the next 20 years.

I'm female, white, middle-aged and have spent my whole life in the middle of America... Wisconsin to be more specific. In this great big global community of Medium's people and ideas, these things are not necessarily important, but they do have relevance. They are relevant because everything I read and write is seen through the lens of my environment and past experience. I want to remain curious and stay open to new ideas and ways of seeing things. I HAVE to stay aware of my brain's tendency to stick to the path of least resistance.

I want to use your lenses along with mine. I want to see things as you see them. I never want to stop asking why. I want to find the middle road and walk with you. Sharing our glasses.

· · ·

When I wrote **Can I Please Try on Your Glasses?** four years ago...

I had no idea how many generous souls would oblige my request.

I had no idea how much existed outside the world and thinking patterns in my brain.

I had no idea that simple words hold different meanings in individual minds.

I had no idea that in this lifetime I'll ever only experience a sugar granule's worth of life's 5-layer chocolate-frosted cake with Ganache and raspberry filling.

I had no idea how difficult it would be dissecting the tight little bud that was ME to make room for what I might become.

I had no idea that from moment to moment I am in flux — still becoming.

"No man ever steps in the same river twice, for it's not the same river and he's not the same man."~Heraclitus

the things one learns
when
airing
out
the
house

We cannot solve our problems with the same level of thinking that created them. ~Albert Einstein

Is humanity stuck in an ineffective way of thinking?

Have we set ourselves up to be knowers rather than learners?

Have we ceded our responsibility for our own growth to gurus and experts?

In *The Rise*, Author Sarah Lewis shares:

Social justice, no matter its kind, comes from more than critique and counterstatement, but from wrestling with seeming failure—what haunts us and what we would rather not inhabit, the gulf between what is and what should be. The tool we marshal to cross our gulf is irrevocably altered vision.

Will you please lend me your glasses?

I am a learner on a quest to alter my vision.

Scaffold Learning

20

TOUCH HEARTS

ove yourself first and everything else falls into line. You really have to love yourself to get anything done in this world. ~Lucille Ball

Mid-August signals the beginning of transition. The daylight hours are taking up a smaller percentage of the daily allotted 24. Swarms of blackbirds have begun migrating through, leaving empty bird feeders in their wake. Stores are advertising bountiful supplies of school essentials awaiting reluctant children and anxious parents.

And then, there is the state fair, signaling summer's last big hurrah.

There is the midway with its Ferris wheel, tilt-a-whirl and pop-the-balloon games. Not a personal favorite of mine, but it does hold allure for many thrill seekers. I think of the life lived by those who travel from place to place, constantly setting up and taking down. Do they like this lifestyle? I am sure some do and some do not, as is the way with all things in life.

We always take a quick stroll through the barns holding the most beautiful cows, sheep, goats, pigs and horses transported from their home farms by hopeful owners, looking for recognition in the form of a ribbon.

This year, as we walked through the barn holding the winners of the governor's auction, I was witness to a touch that touched me. All of the animals are kept in immaculate pens and tended to by their owners as mobs of people walk through taking in the sights and atmosphere.

I saw a young man seated outside of the pen of the above pictured winning sheep. He was talking to a pretty young woman who was sitting on a stool nearby. I watched as the sheep, very dog-like in its action, approached his young master and extended his neck seeking a pat on the head. Absentmindedly, the young man reached out and gave the creature a pat and a scratch.

It really wasn't much of anything, but it struck a chord with me. This tiny bit of affection and connection that passed between the sheep and his boy... it is magic written about in books and portrayed in movies. All living things are connected.

We carried on with our usual rounds, viewing winning photos and decorated cakes. We watched brave (or crazy) people catapulted hundreds of feet into the air on a seat attached to massive bungee-like cords. We ate baked potatoes, sausages, deep fried clam strips and cream puffs. All traditions we have kept over the last 15 years.

But it was that one moment, that one touch that left an impression on me. I imagine not another soul thought twice about it, including the young man and the sheep. It is amazing what you can see in the smallest details if only you keep your eyes open. Life is constant transition. It is the connection that makes it meaningful.

"If only you could sense how important you are to the lives of those you meet; how important you can be to people you may never even dream of. There is something of yourself that you leave at every meeting with another person." ~ Fred Rogers

"Don't ask yourself what the world needs, ask yourself what makes you come alive. And then go and do that. Because what the world needs is people who have come alive." ~Howard Washington Thurman

Touch Hearts

21

UNDERSTAND

*B*oth my father and father-in-law suffer from hearing loss. Each handles it in his own way. One nods his head a lot and the other becomes frustrated when he can't understand — his eyes squint, lips purse, and I always envision steam coming out of his ears.

Yesterday I met my father and his friend Jean at a restaurant for lunch. When I pulled into the parking lot fifteen minutes early, I found them already parked and waiting for me. We all got out of our vehicles and shared hugs before entering through the restaurant's door with a bell. While Jean gazed at pies under glass, my dad and I scanned the joint for our favorite waitress, Mary.

"I don't see her, Dad," I said.

"Me neither. Maybe she's not working today," he replied. If he were a balloon, you would have seen him deflating. We'd specifically chosen a Wednesday meeting because on one of our visits, Mary teased my dad as we were leaving. She called, "Next time come on a Monday or Tuesday... Those are my days off!"

My 82-year-old father's never forgotten and we've never gone to eat there on a Monday or Tuesday.

The hostess seated us and the waitress we'd had on our last visit approached our table for drink orders. She's pleasant, speaks loudly for my father and tries to be accommodating. Later, when my dad ordered meatloaf and she told him they were out, he replied, "Well, we'll just go to Applebees then!"

She handled it as best she could by pointing out pork chops and roast turkey on the senior menu, but my dad's face still wore a frown. *Did I see a few wisps of steam escape before he settled on the chops?*

If Mary had been our waitress, she would have razzed my dad right back. She might have said something like *Let me drive you over* or *You still owe me a tip for that water I just brought.* Both would have laughed and my dad would have ordered the chops with a smile.

Mary understands my dad *and* she's got the skills to coax the best out of him.

My chair faced the swinging doors to the kitchen. As we waited for our food, I smiled when I saw Mary come out with a tray balanced on her right hand. She headed to another part of the dining room. I knew if she swung by our table the air would lighten and I could eat my southwest chicken salad without fear of indigestion.

My dad spied her as she made her way back to the kitchen. "Hello!" he called out.

"Well hello — it's been a while," she replied with a twinkle. "Just let me finish up with another table and I'll stop back."

True to her word, she came over between taking and delivering orders. We shared a light conversation and she and Dad bantered a bit. Mary admired a photo of my son holding a 36-inch brown trout and told us about her grandkids in Oregon. When my dad's eyes squinted and lips began to purse because he couldn't figure out how Mary drove to Oregon and back in one weekend, she metered her sentences and enunciated every syllable to let him know her grandkids live in Oregon, *Wisconsin*, a suburb of Madison.

My dad can be a tough nut, but Mary doesn't let it faze her. For some unknown reason, she understands and pushes all the right buttons.

I'll bet she makes out pretty good on tips.

Understand

22

VALUE TRUTH

This morning as I lifted shovel upon shovel full of snow to shoulder height or above, I pondered whether I was working with the highest snowbanks to ever surround our drive. *Gotta be* I thought. *The exposed tips of our burning bush branches*

are no longer than my fingers — and the bush is as big as it's ever been.

I've yet to share my analysis with my fellow driveway shovelers. There's a possibility they won't agree with what I believe. Truth on this mountainous point is elusive and subjective. We've never kept measurements. If there's photographic evidence, we'll never find it. We have over 25 discs with photos spanning ten years or more. Some of them have eight pictures, while others record hundreds of snaps. Looking back at yearly snowfall totals won't be helpful — we can't account for melting and settling from season to season, *right?*

I value truth.

When I feel or sense somebody is playing it straight with me, I trust — sometimes without empirical evidence. It's gotten me into trouble a time or two... a chance I'm usually willing to take.

What I've learned to keep in mind is that a lot of **truth** is built on our past experience and future expectations.

Truth can be tricky. Have you heard that some scientific experiments find exactly what researchers are looking for? And then another experiment on the same subject yields completely different answers when conducted by another researcher — possibly with different expectations.

It's really tough for us to step away from what hides

in our unconscious. Perhaps that's why they blindfold subjects who taste test Coke vs. Pepsi?

All of the pieces don't always add up to what we expect.

So... what if a lot of truth is simply what we can agree upon?

Is the dress *gold and white* or *blue and black*? Are the snowbanks record breakers? Who is the best quarter-back ever? Sweetest dog breed? Organic versus conventional?

Sometimes the best we can do is agree to disagree while working towards harmony. Consider evidence with rational thought and logic. Recognize the other guy sees something you don't see. Work toward middle ground...

Because a lot of truth is simply what we can agree upon.

Value Truth

23

WIN GRACIOUSLY

haracter is like a tree and reputation its shadow.
The shadow is what we think of it; the tree is the
real thing. ~Abraham Lincoln

I've never met the tree. Her name is Eva. I have seen
her shadow, though. It overtook me in the form of an
email message. The shadow (actually more of a light)
appeared in my inbox as part of an email chain, refer-
encing a speedskating competition.

The race Eva references was a marathon — 130 laps around an Olympic sized oval — 26.2 miles. Simply attempting such a feat speaks of character. To win fairly and then gracefully ask to step aside so that somebody else receives recognition speaks of integrity, honesty, respect, and fairness — **character amplified.**

(The email's author has given me permission to share. Full names have been reduced to initials.)

Dear GS,

Thank you, and to all the officials and volunteers, for all your hard work in hosting this great event!

I wanted to send this email as a reply to the results link, because I am worried that a mistake I made, in signing up for the wrong division, has cost another skater a well-deserved record in her appropriate category. It's easy enough to find the information that I'm 40 years old, yet I signed up for the "open" division, which is a bit confusing because this is also known as the "19–29" age division. This is 100% my fault, because B sent the spreadsheet around for us to edit in the week leading up to the race, but I neglected to correct this. Partly because I got busy with work and blew it off, and partly because, well...maybe I didn't want to admit I was in a Masters age group?

Anyway: I believe that RJ deserves to have the record in the women's 19–29 age division. She skated an absolutely incredible race, and I feel that she should have her name and her time recognized. I don't know if it's possible to move me into the 40–49 age group where I belong, retroactively, but I just wanted to put in my two cents on this. It's rare for skaters who are training for elite (mostly middle-distance) races to come out and skate a marathon, and I would hate for any skater to have a bad experience just because I made a careless mistake on my registration.

My apologies for spamming the entire group on this, but I would like to hear input from other competitors as well, if you feel like supporting this change.

Thanks and kind regards,

Eva

I was taken with Eva's courage in sharing her respectful and authentic request with all who competed in the marathon.

The world is full of humans displaying character every day. After reading Eva's message, I wanted you to share in the feeling her words gave me. I set my untethered fingers to the task of connecting with Eva — a tree casting a shadow worth seeing.

Character encompasses core ethical values that transcend religious, cultural, socioeconomic and political differences. Eva's email speaks volumes and, therefore, I'll simply leave you with one more thought:

"Waste no more time arguing what a good man should be. Be one." ~Marcus Aurelius

Win Graciously

24

XERISCAPE

I had to look up xeriscape — *again.*

Xeriscaping is gardening without irrigation. Think rocks and succulents.

I've never lived in an arid climate but have been fortunate to visit Arizona a number of times. Serious xeriscapers can work magic with hunks of sandstone and cacti. I wonder if there are special xeriscaping gloves? Protection from needles and scorpions?

Last summer I visited a Japanese garden in Rockford, Illinois. There were trees and mosses surrounded by lots of gravel. Boulders and Asian architecture added punch to the scenery. I watched a xeriscaper rake a bed of pebbles, leaving Zen patterns behind. Signs around the garden requested visitors keep their feet on designated paths — so as not to disturb the xeriscaping I suppose.

I recently learned about a guy named Norman Borlaug. He was an American agronomist and humanitarian who collaborated with scientists from Mexico, India and Pakistan. He doesn't technically meet the definition of a xeriscaper, but he won the Nobel Prize in 1970 for his work hybridizing wheat and corn so that they'd flourish in arid climates. Borlaug sought to reduce deforestation by increasing crop yields. He was an above average achiever.

Author Andy Andrews credits Borlaug's efforts with saving two billion lives from starvation in his book *The Butterfly Effect*.

You, too, can get your hands dirty.

Helping something grow is as satisfying as munching buttered popcorn while watching Little Shop of Horrors. The whole world is a garden with climates as varied as its inhabitants.

So — xeriscape or garden. Raise a cactus or a plum tree — a Labrador retriever or a child.

None of it will do exactly what you expect, but that's half of the fun.

Xeriscape

25

YEARN FOR PEACE

*T*he lot was only half full.

"Where is everyone?" I asked my husband. "Remember last year? We had trouble finding a parking spot."

Standing behind our Tahoe, we pulled our feet out of winter boots and slid them into ski boots. We slipped our cross country skis and poles over the collapsed truck seats, walked over to the mattress-sized, wooden trail map and contemplated how far we were willing to slide on our first trek of the season.

"Brown is less than a mile — white just over three. Can we split the difference and take the purple?" I asked.

"Sounds good."

"If that's not enough for you, I'll sit in the warming shack while you add on the brown, okay? Or maybe I'll want to go, too!"

"We'll see," he replied.

The groomed Nordic loops are part of the Kettle Moraine State Forest, a geographic feature left behind by receding glaciers. The Nordic park is located directly across the road from the John Muir hiking and biking trails. I'm so grateful to live in an area where nature is accessible and abundant.

We set our ski clad feet into four parallel grooves and began moving arms and legs in a graceful dance. Within several hundred yards, I found I was coaching myself.

Stop gripping your poles so fiercely! Relax your legs! You're holding tension and expending energy in places that are not propelling you forward. Clenching your jaw does not help you to ski! The sooner you relax, the more fun you'll have.

I shocked myself with my own coaching abilities! I

began to let go in all the right places, making room to absorb sights, smells and sounds.

When we came upon the scene pictured above, the beauty and tranquility grabbed me. "I didn't bring my phone, will you take a picture?" I called. "I love the thought of what wonders await in the foggy unknown."

We never found out as our trail curved, taking us in another direction. Perhaps I'll revisit that spot in summer. If I can figure out what direction we were facing, it'd be fun to try to capture a sunrise or sunset in the mysterious gap.

Now...

*Can we talk about the word **yearn** for a minute?* If you've been reading along as I walk and write about the ABCs of living, it won't surprise you that I have a contrary thought to this letter's directive.

yearn = *have an intense feeling of longing for something, typically something that one has lost or been separated from*

I used to *yearn for peace*.

I thought peace was something outside of myself. I'd watch the news, or attend a family gathering, or read comments on social media and long for everyone to get along — or at a minimum, tolerate each other.

What I've finally come to grasp is that I cannot control circumstances or other people. What I can control is my reaction. This message has been presented to me in hundreds of places — written, spoken, sung, experienced. *What took me so long to catch on?*

I no longer *yearn for peace* because I've found it.

Peace is inside of me. With every interaction, I try to share some. That's my circle of influence. Simple.

Peace is inside of you, too.

My wish is that you find it because, when you do, the world becomes a better place.

Yearn for Peace

26

ZEALOUSLY SUPPORT A WORTHY CAUSE

All that we are is a result of what we have thought.
~Buddha

The road to the letter Z has taken me 25 letters and fifty years.

So, *zealously support a worthy cause*?

What **should** that cause be? Scratch that.

What **could** that cause be?

I'll not answer for you, but I do have a suggestion...

You are worthy.

Are you supporting yourself?

Do you surround yourself with people, ideas, images, music and activities that lift and fill you?

Because everything flows from there...

"Keep my words positive:
>*Words become my behaviors.*
>*Keep my behaviors positive:*
>*Behaviors become my habits.*
>*Keep my habits positive:*
>*Habits become my values.*
>*Keep my values positive:*
>*Values become my destiny.*
>*There is no dress rehearsal:*
>*This is one day in your life."*
~Mohandas K. Gandhi

Every interaction is an opportunity to lift someone up or tear them down. This includes the conversations you have with yourself — about yourself.

You cannot load your trunk with rocks, point your car downhill, and expect it to climb.

Notice what makes you feel bad — and stop carrying it.

Every joyful person lifts us all.

I don't know what lights your candle, but I write to share what's lit mine.

Now... where are those matches?

Zealously Support a Worthy Cause

EPILOGUE

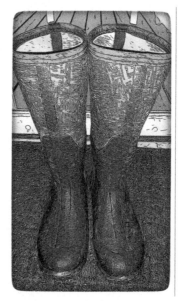

*a*n analogy for love?
What a playful question!
I replied...

Love is like my knee-high rubber boots in spring. They are reliable, keep my feet warm and dry, and understand when I wear another pair of shoes. They are not flashy or showy...they simply get the job done.

What did you mean when you said, "... they understand when I wear another pair of shoes?"

I used to be a jealous person — afraid of being left behind. Thankfully I am past that phase.

True love makes space for growth and exploration... it does not cling or try to control.

I guess that's **not** what I learned about love while watching *As the World Turns* and *The Guiding Light* — dramatic soap operas make poor role models.

...

Giving and receiving LOVE is like my knee-high rubber boots in spring...

Love gives me the courage to go places
I wouldn't dare go,
Without it.

ACKNOWLEDGMENTS

*Like flower fluff, we send our seeds and they look for
fertile ground.*

If I were to acknowledge from A to Z everyone who
helped create me, who in turn created this book, the
pages would roll on into infinity.

I simply cannot do it.

Even though it feels like a cop-out, my greatest life learning is that every experience and person that I connect with has co-created "me"...

From the butterfly Henrietta chases on the cover to the encouragers who never once gave up on me — who saw beauty and potential I could not see in myself...

I offer love and heartfelt gratitude.

No kidding... tears pricked my eyes as I wrote this page.

Thank you.

AFTERWORD

It has been nearly five years since I started writing and publishing an almost daily blog/newsletter. About a year ago a friend asked me if I would ever write a book.

My response went something like, "If I wrote a book now, it would just be an attempt to feed my ego."

What was that about?

Looking back, the material shared in this book was all written and available at the time he asked. What held me back was not ego, but fear — I was still wearing a heavy wool coat of insecurity.

Who am I to write a book? I wondered.

Today I ask myself, *Who are you to NOT write a book?*

I hope the stories I share here inspire you to coax your mouse onto the boat.

Courage is fed by those who surround you, so choose wisely.

Baby steps or leaping bounds, what matters is the choice to keep going.

NEXT UP? MEANDERING MUSES

Popcorn? That's strange.

I bent down to pick up the perfectly shaped, yellow-white anomaly from the hallway floor.

I'd just come in from filling bird feeders with seed,

and deer feeder with cracked corn. The floor had been swept and mopped minutes before I went outside.

How did that popcorn get there? Nobody else is home.

All of this ran through my mind as I walked the short distance between garage entry and kitchen. Upon the table there was a beautifully wrapped box. It carried a tag, addressing the gift to me.

To: Gail

From: U, T, & C

U, T, & C? Who, what??? I was only outside for minutes. Confusion and curiosity left only one course — open the box.

The interior was packed with envelopes neatly divided into four sections.

Three sections wore labels: Memories, New Adventures, People You Will Meet. The fourth stack of envelopes was free of distinction.

An envelope was affixed to the box lid with black corner tabs; the kind used in old photo albums to hold pictures in place. One word said *simply* — **open**.

The calligraphy read:

Dear Gail,

Until now, we've kept our presence a secret. We are your muses, Urania, Thalia, and Calliope.

We took you by the hand last spring and

encouraged you to tell your stories. We found a safe place for you to share your words, making sure there was abundant support to encourage and guide you.

We see that our judgement was good. We are pleased with your progress and effort.

Today, we felt it was time to make our presence and expectations known.

There is responsibility in telling stories. Of course, the process of getting ideas out of your head and onto the page is for you. By all means, write for yourself, but — your published work must be written for an audience. Words and stories are among the most powerful weapons ever created. They can fight for good or bad. Use them wisely, with good intent.

This box contains stories you have lived. That is the stack labeled memories.

There are stacks of envelopes pertaining to future experiences and people you will meet. We will make sure you will always have ideas to work with.

The unlabeled stack, well, that's the unknown. The unknown leaves space to grow into. For you, it might be fiction or poetry one day.

This gift is real but only exists in your thoughts. The physical box and envelopes are an illusion. The gift lies within your heart and mind.

You've got potential. We'll always be nearby. If

we do not come when you call, it is because you need to think a little longer — or possibly, we've run out for more popcorn.

Love and inspiration to you,

U, T, & C

ABOUT THE AUTHOR

Taking the slow lane and enjoying the walk

Gail Boenning is an emerging author of creative non-fiction short stories — while leaving space for any squirrels that cross her path. Poetry? Fiction? Song writing? Who knows?

> *"We will discover the nature of our particular genius when we stop trying to conform to our own or other people's models, learn to be ourselves, and allow our natural channel to open."* ~Shakti Gawain

Gail recognizes her life is in large part a reflection of what she chooses to see. With this awareness, she looks for the best in everything and everyone who crosses her path believing that energy flows to the places we give our attention.

What gets recognized gets repeated.